Flower Painting With Watercolor

Beautiful Art Projects With Watercolor For Beginners

Copyright © 2021

All rights reserved.

DEDICATION

The author and publisher have provided this e-book to you for your personal use only. You may not make this e-book publicly available in any way. Copyright infringement is against the law. If you believe the copy of this e-book you are reading infringes on the author's copyright, please notify the publisher at: https://us.macmillan.com/piracy

Contents

BASIC FLOWER 1

FORSYTHIAS 28

EASY WATERCOLOR FLOWERS 35

MAKE BUBBLE PAINT FLOWER HYDRANGEAS 58

Basic Flower

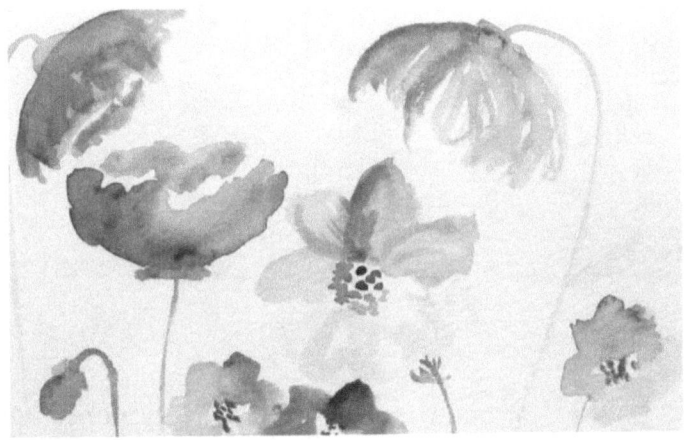

Watercolor is my favorite painting medium to work with because it's so fluid and organic. At the same time, it can also be unpredictable and unforgiving, so don't be too hard on yourself if you can't seem to paint what you want. Part of the fun is letting the watercolors have control and just watching what comes out of the brush. Keep in mind that your own artistic style will emerge when you try this tutorial, and that is what's so awesome about making art!

To get started, here are the supplies that you'll need:

Flower Painting With Watercolor

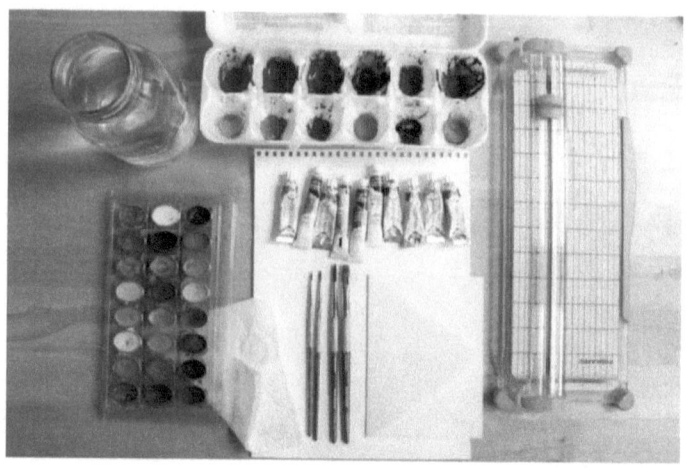

A jar or tub of water

Watercolor paints (Crayola works just fine! Their bigger set on the left contains some beautiful vivid colors for less than $4. Also note that Styrofoam egg cartons make awesome palettes.)

Watercolor paper (I prefer 140 lb weight 9"x11" pads. The thicker the paper, the less likely it is to warp.)

Envelopes if you're making note cards

Brushes (My favorites are sizes 0, 2, and 6 round brushes)

A paper towel to soak up excess water and paint

Optional: a paper cutter

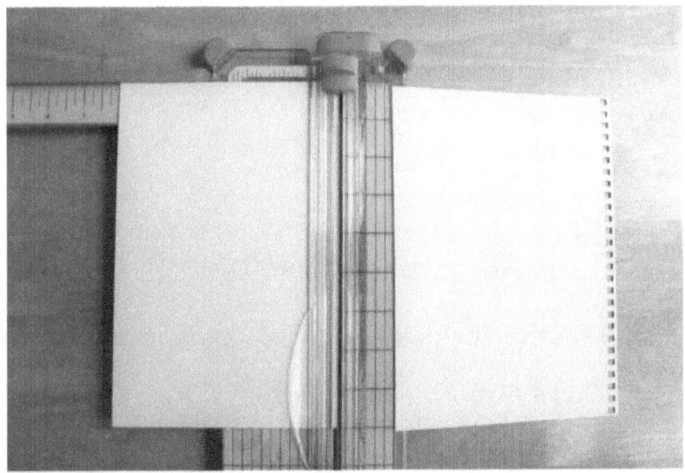

Step 1: Cut your paper into the sizes you want to work with. You can use scissors if you don't have a paper cutter. I cut mine into 6" by 8" pieces to fold into 4" by 6" note cards. I like making 4×6's because they're easy to stick in a small frame!

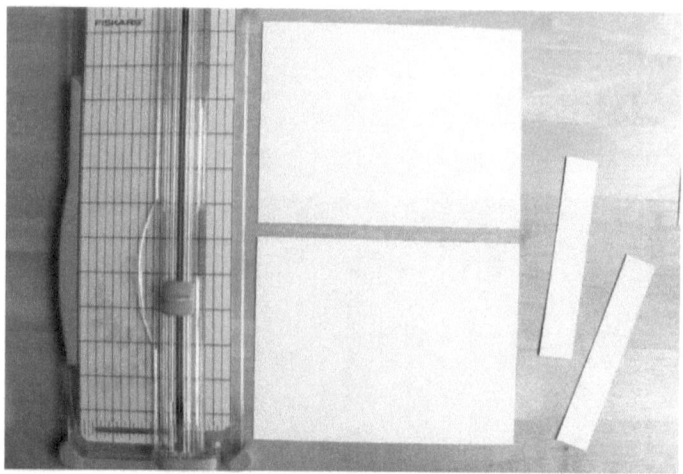

The 9×12 inch watercolor pad makes two cards per page with some scraps leftover that I turn into bookmarks.

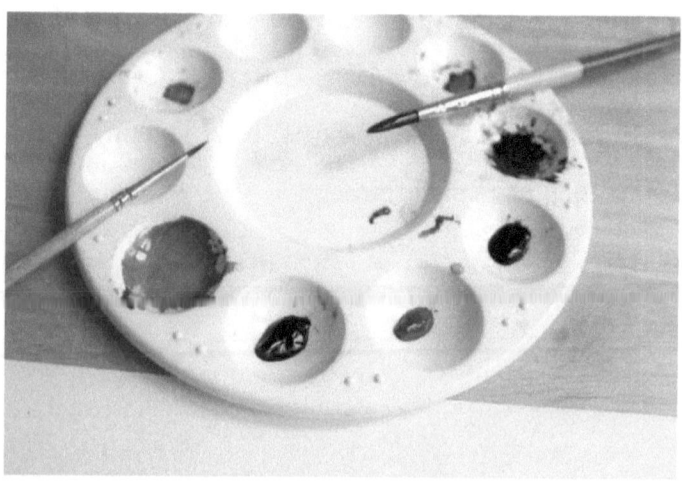

Step 2: Choose the colors you want to use. For this tutorial I'm going to use (from left to right between the brushes) yellow-green, dark purple, pink, magenta, and dark blue. You can use whatever colors you want, but I recommend choosing 2-4 shades that are next to each other on the color wheel for the flowers, and some sort of green for the leaves and stems.

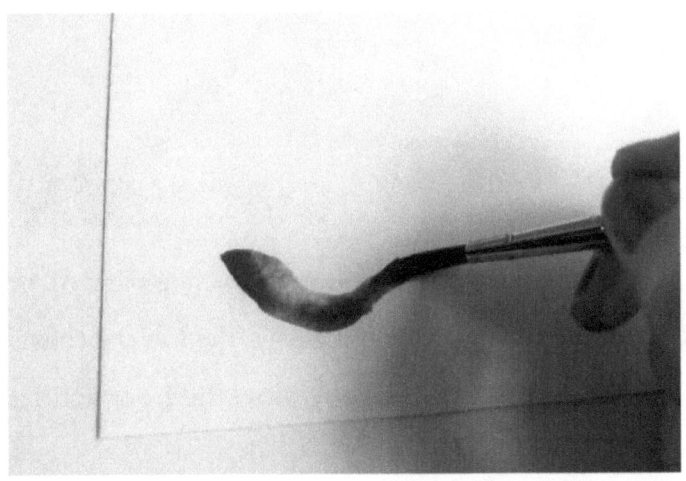

Step 3: First I'll show you how to paint a poppy-esque flower. Dip a medium size round brush (I'm using #6) into water, pick up some of the dark blue paint, and start by painting a U shape.

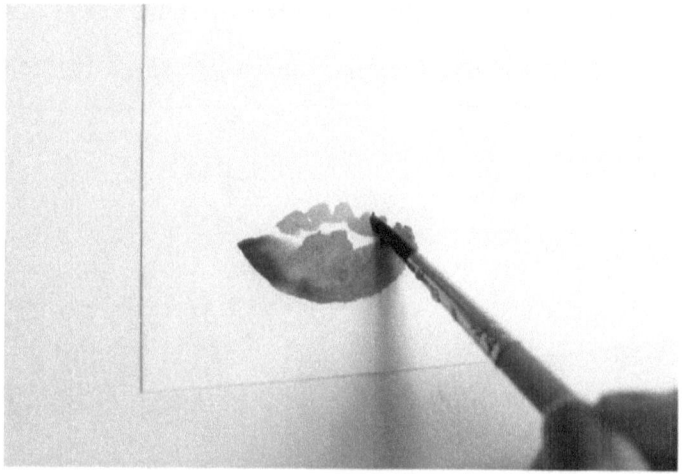

Step 4: Fill in the U shape so it looks like a side view of petals, and then paint a thinner squiggly shape above the lower petals, leaving a very thin white space between what is now the front and back petals of the flower.

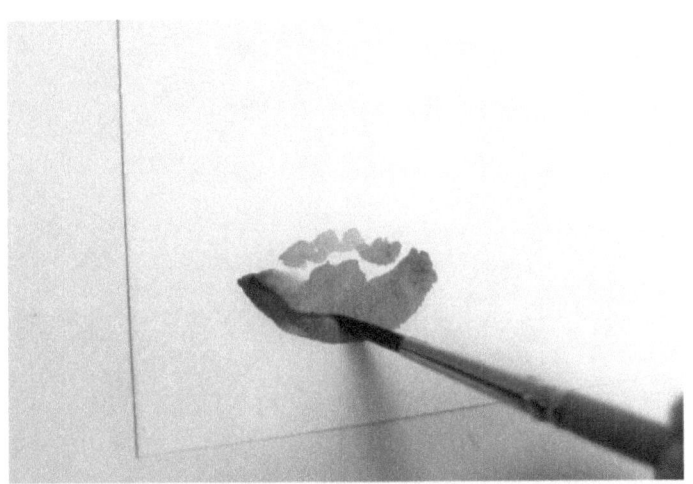

Step 5: Before your first flower has a chance to dry, quickly clean your brush in water and pick up some contrasting paint (I'm using purple now). Dab the contrasting color along the bottom of the flower and allow it to bleed into the blue for a shaded effect. If the color comes on too dark you can blot it with a paper towel for a different effect. Play with it!

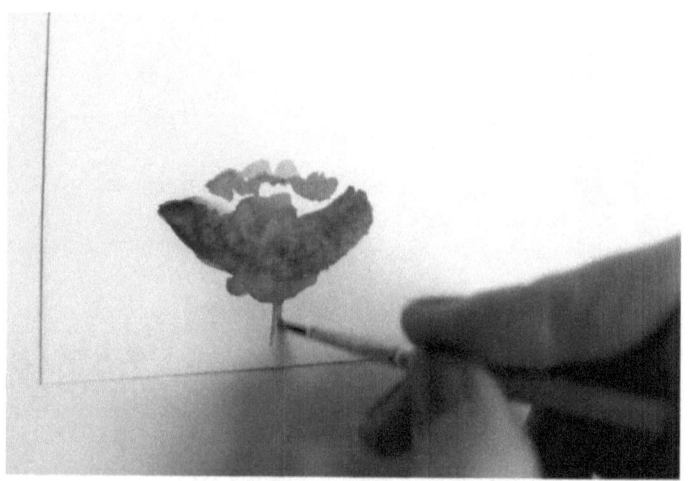

Step 6: Using your smallest brush, pick up some green paint and add a blob of green to the bottom of the flower. Again, let the paint bleed into the petals if it's still wet. In a delicate, quick motion, draw a line down from the flower for the stem.

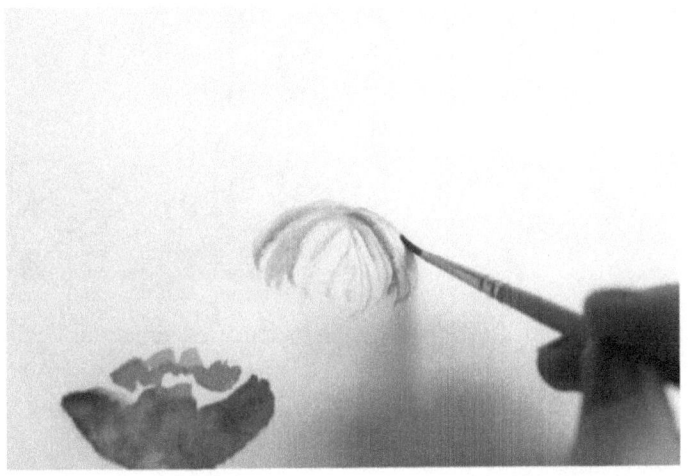

Step 7: Now let's make a different flower. This one looks like a thistle or spider mum. I'm using some of the magenta paint and the smallest brush (#0). Quickly swipe the paint down in curved lines from one central point, in an umbrella shape. Pick up more water and paint as your brush will dry out after two or three swipes.

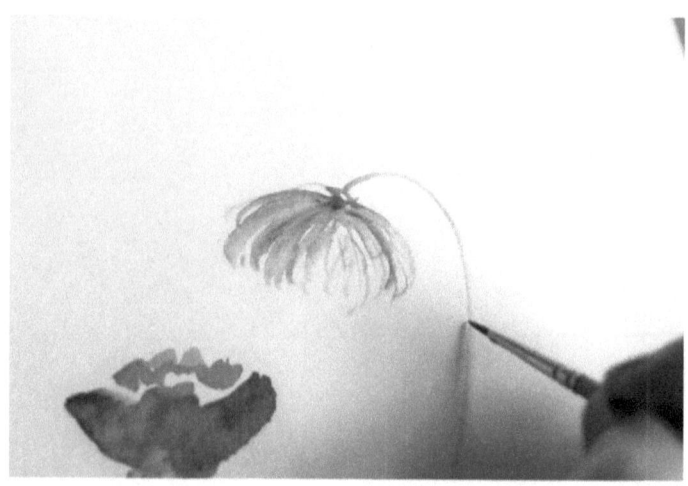

Step 8: In green, add a curving stem to the flower, again using a very quick and light sweep of the smallest brush.

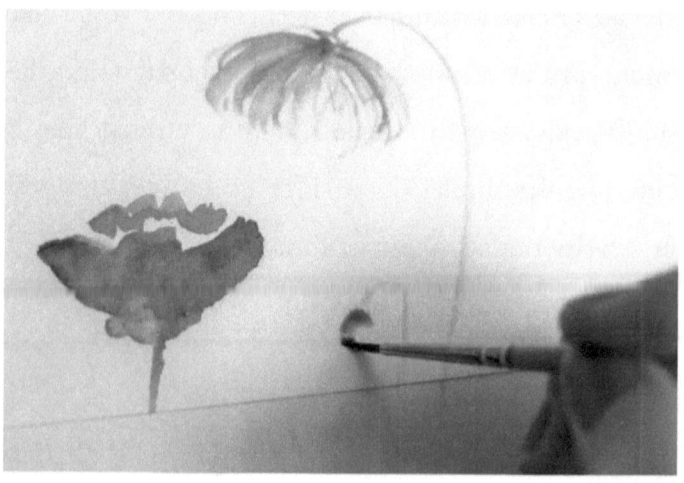

Step 9: Now let's have a Bob Ross moment and make a happy little

flower bud. Draw a curving stem and then in blue paint a little blob at the end of the stem.

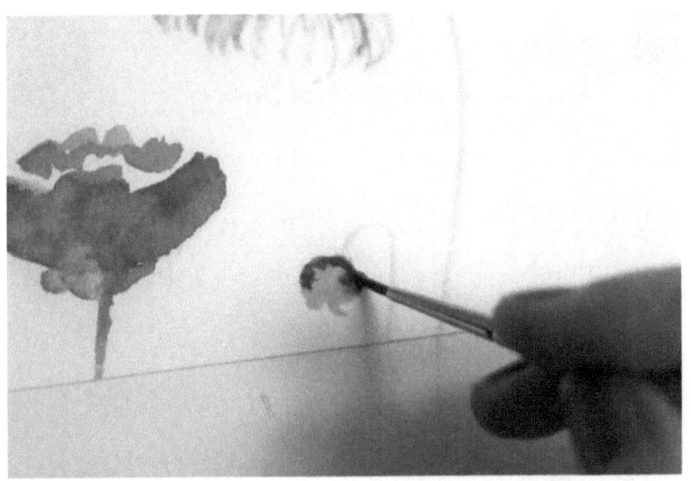

Step 10: With purple, add a dot of contrasting purple to the bud. Mine was very dark so I blotted it with a paper towel.

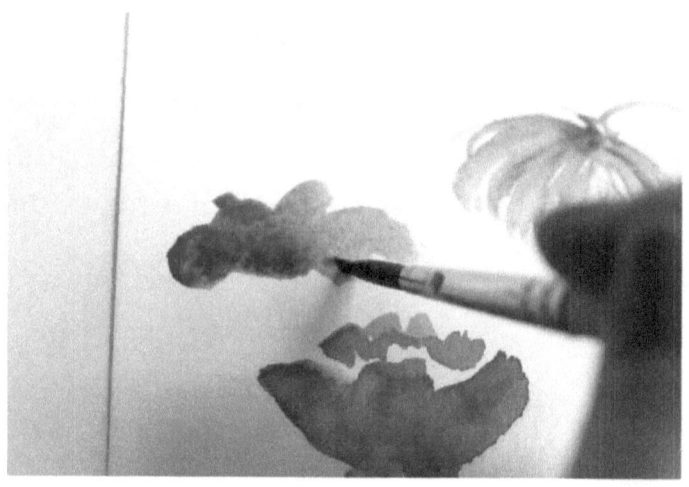

Step 11: Next I painted another poppy flower in blue and purple, using similar technique as the very first flower. I made a different shape though. Experiment!

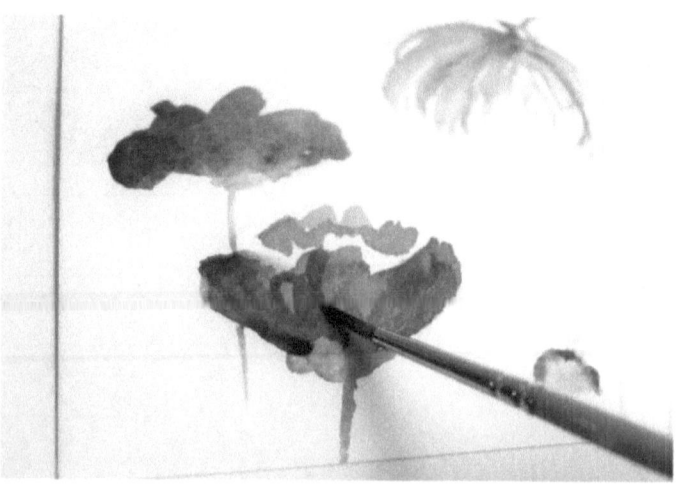

Step 12: After the flowers have dried, you can go back with a small

brush and add some detail to the petals.

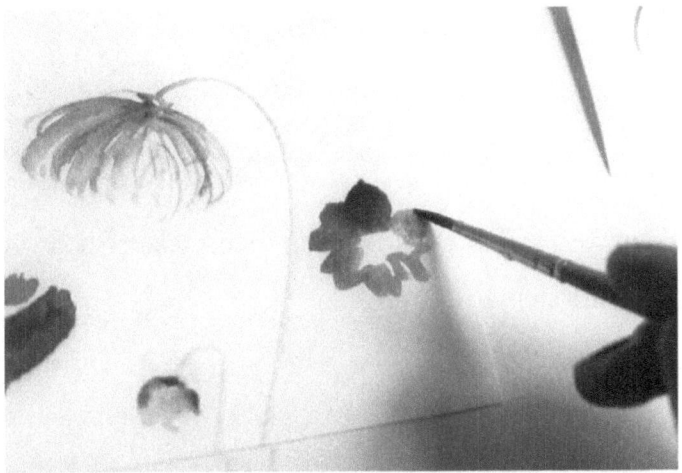

Step 13: I decided to add one more flower, a small blue one. I painted a basic front-facing flower shape in blue and then blotted it with a paper towel.

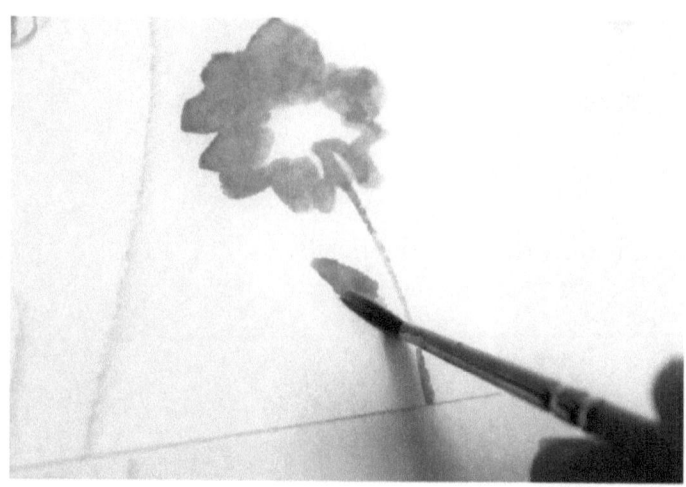

Step 14: To make a leaf, press down and then back up with your brush, connecting to the stem.

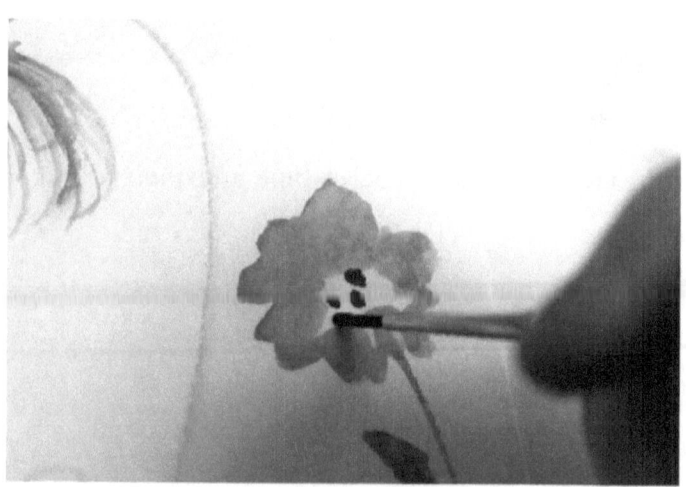

Step 15: I added some more detail to the flower after it was dry by

painting dark dots in the center.

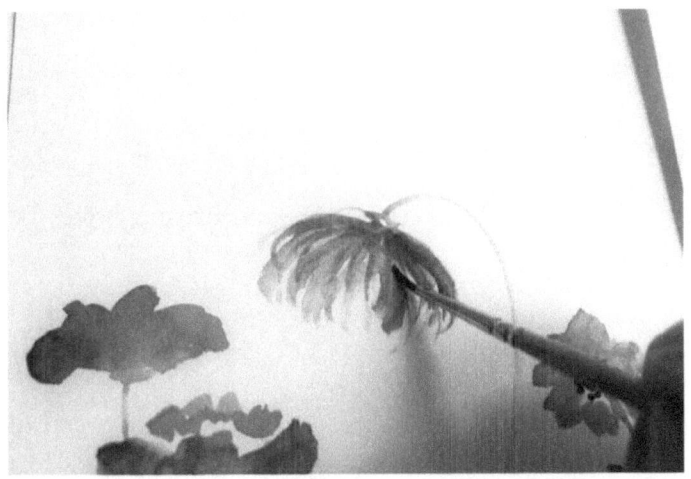

Step 16: My magenta flower was looking a little sparse so I went back and filled it in with some more color.

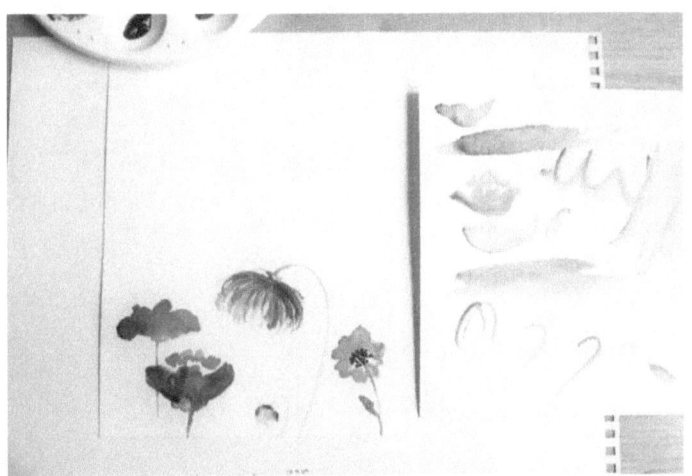

Voila! The finished product! Note my piece of scrap paper on the side. It's handy to have a place to test colors and brush strokes before you take your brush to the actual work!

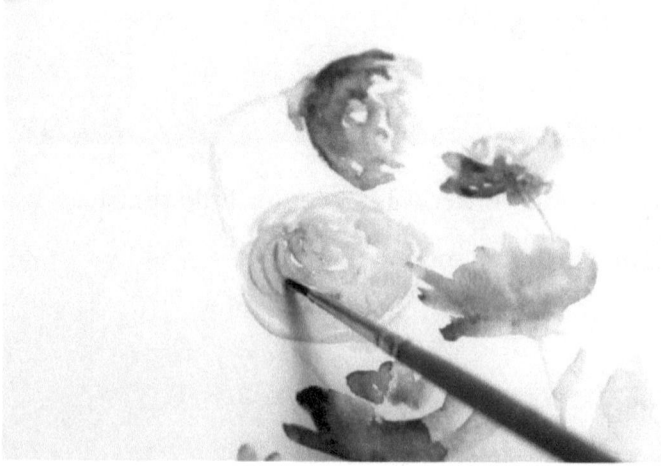

Extra Credit: To paint roses or peonies, make "C" shapes out from a central point with a small brush, making the "C's" bigger as you extend out from the center.

Flower Painting With Watercolor

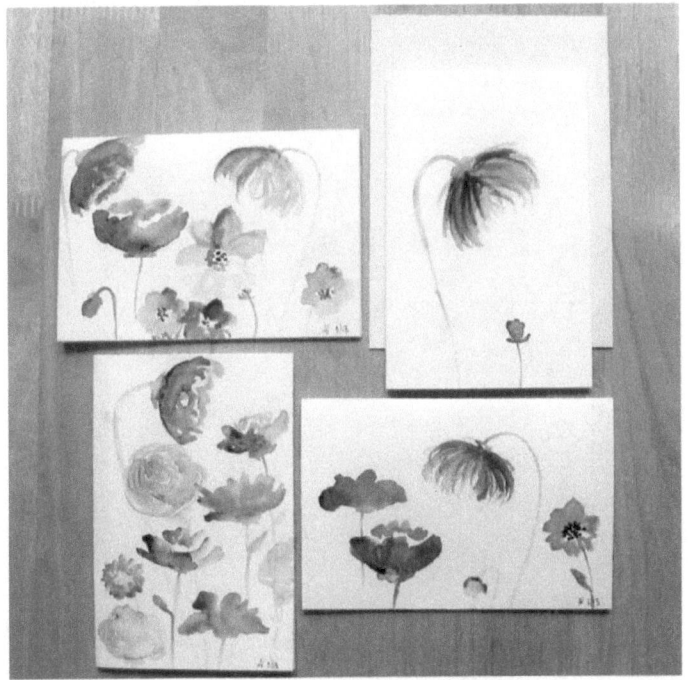

Flower Rubber Cement Resist

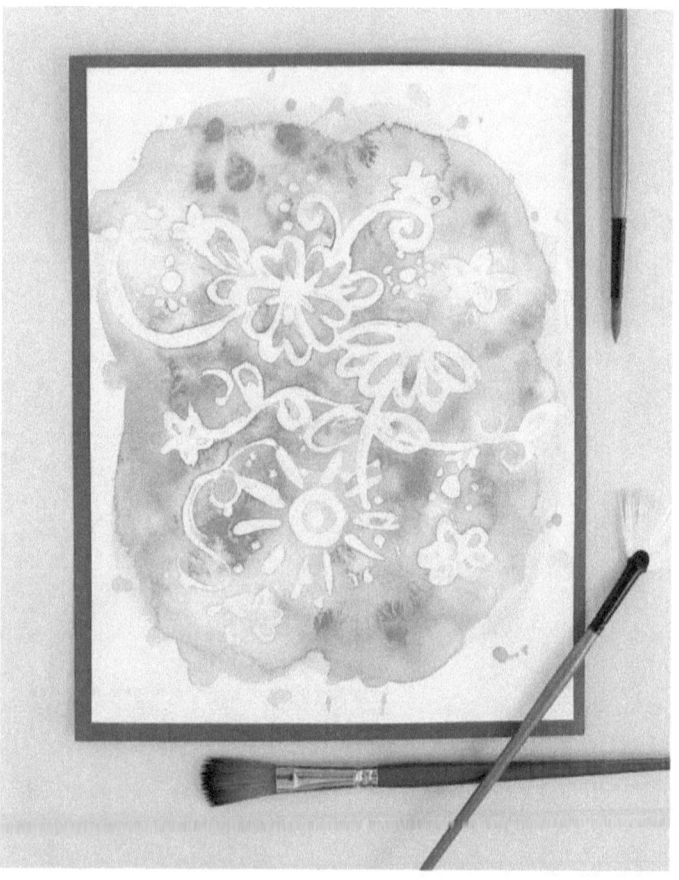

Watercolors are so fun because of the way they interact with and react to other media. I have already put watercolors with plastic wrap and salt, but today we are bringing in a whole new element. This guy:

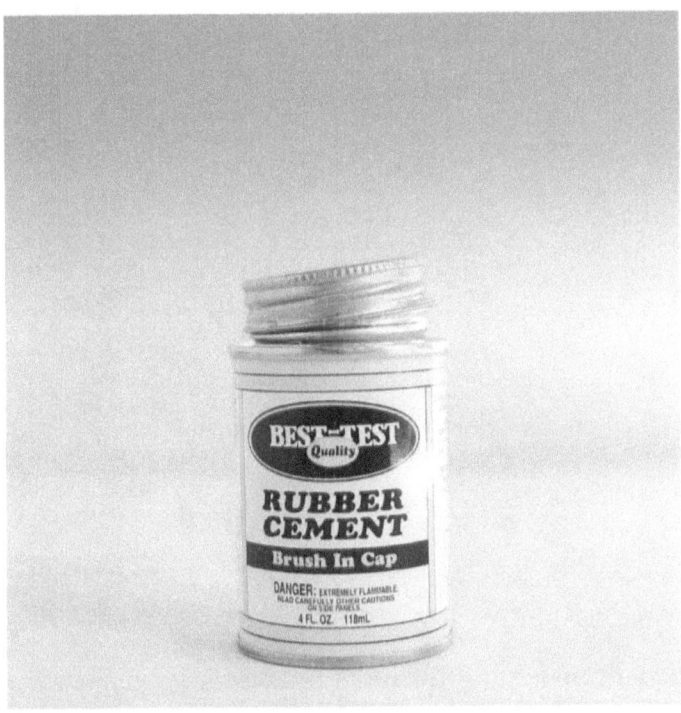

Look familiar? That's right! It's humble rubber cement, that fun goopy, sticky stuff with the brush in the lid you probably remember using as a kid. Today we are going to use rubber cement to make a resist painting, which is when you use two mediums that don't get along well to create designs, patterns, and texture. With watercolors, often you start by laying down a design onto your paper using a resist medium (something that watercolor doesn't play well with) and then painting over that with your watercolors. The paint won't adhere to the paper where the medium is, and then when you remove it, you have a beautiful watercolor design!

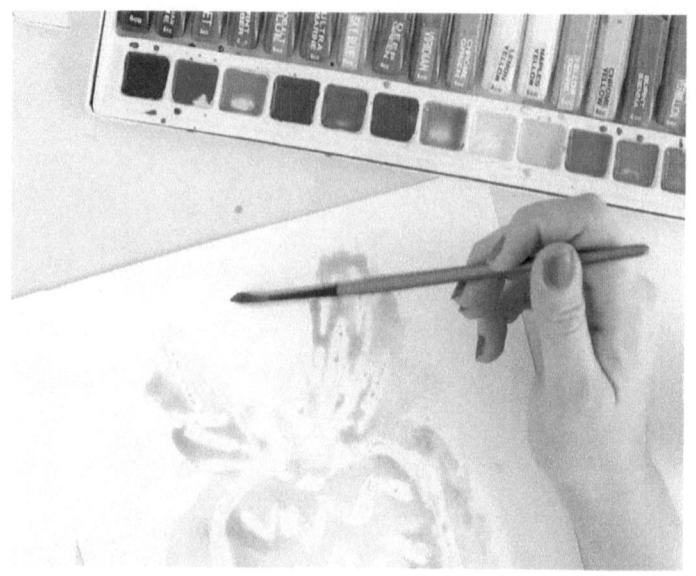

Rubber cement makes a great resist because it is inexpensive, easy to find, and easily removable. Plus, you will feel like a kid again when you are using it! So, it's pretty much the best. Ready to make some beautiful and easy watercolor art paintings? Let's do this!

EASY WATERCOLOR ART SUPPLIES:

Watercolor Paper

Watercolors – Tube or Pan

Watercolor Brushes (round brushes are my favorites)

Small, Inexpensive Round Brush (for the rubber cement)

Rubber Cement

Pencil (optional)

Quality Eraser

Step One – Paint Resist Design

Start off by painting your design onto the watercolor paper with rubber cement and a small round brush. It can be a little bit difficult to see where you have painted, but the rubber cement has a sheen to it, so picking up the paper and holding it at different angles can help you to see it.

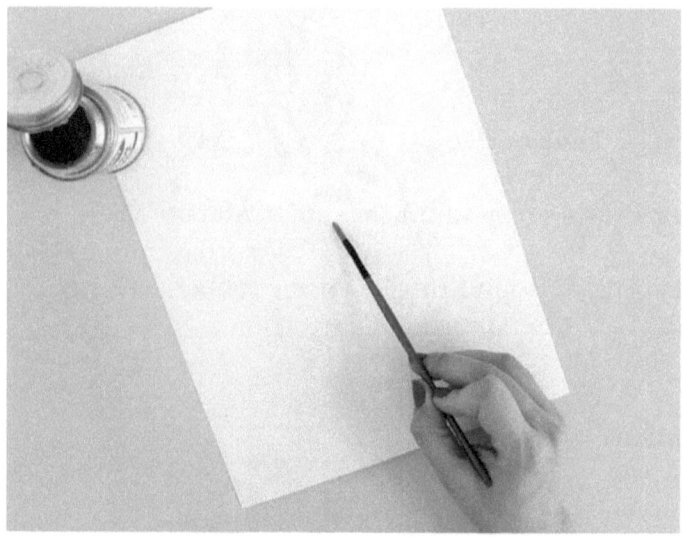

To get the best result, you really need to use quite a bit of rubber cement. If you apply it too thinly there will be holes that will let the watercolor through to the paper. Just load up that brush with rubber cement and reload often.

I freehanded my designs, and I really like the painterly look they have, but if you don't feel comfortable doing that, you can trace a design lightly onto your paper with pencil and fill it in with rubber cement.

When you are done with your resist design, set it aside to dry.

Step Two – Prepare your Palette

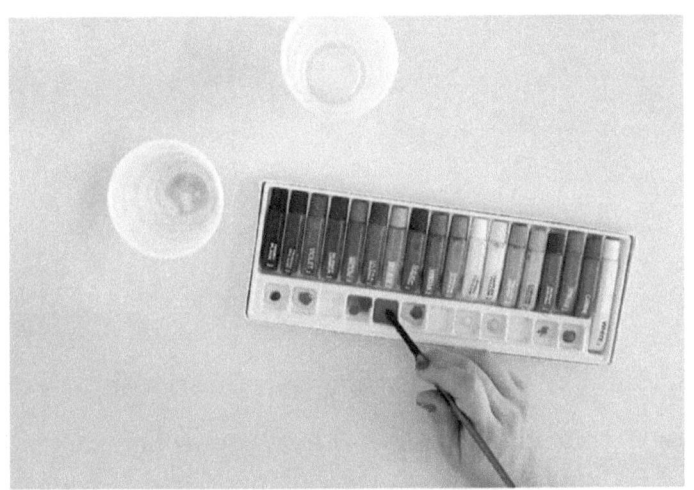

While your rubber cement is drying, it's time to prep your palette. If you are using tube colors like I used, just squirt a little drop of paint onto your palette and use your brush to mix in some water to get the color and opaqueness you want. Feel free to mix and create your own custom colors. Once your palette is ready and your rubber cement design is dry, you are ready to paint.

Step Three – Paint!

This is the fun part! Start by loading your brush with watercolor and painting over your entire design. Add water to lighten the color or more pigment to darken it. Try adding in areas or drops of analogous or contrasting colors.

Flower Painting With Watercolor

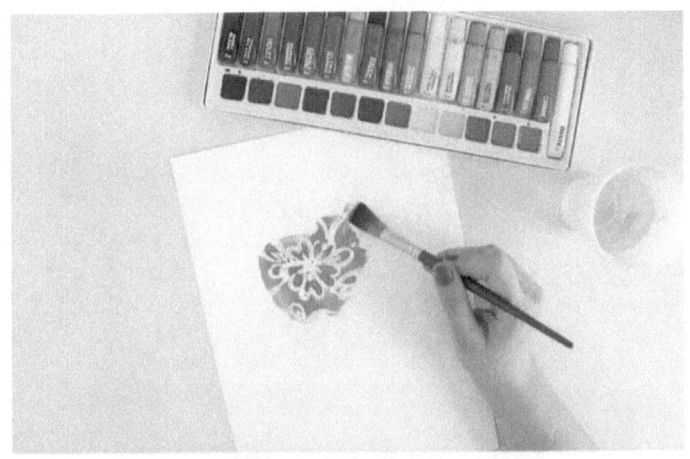

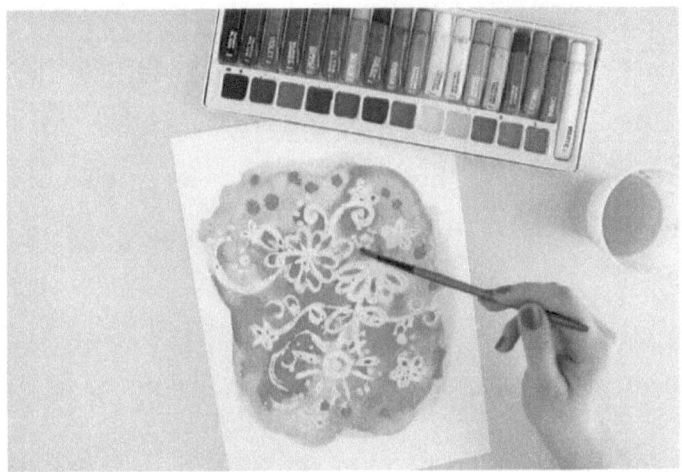

It's so much fun to see your design revealed as you paint! I painted this floral design with reds, yellows, and purples. Here's how it turned out:

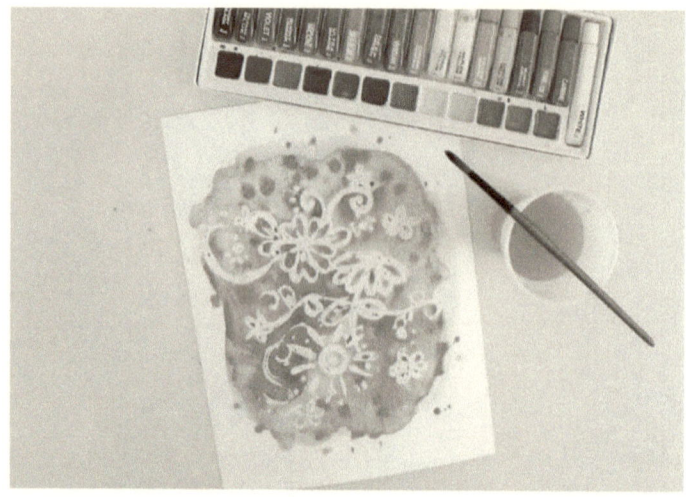

I really love the look of some watercolor splatter around the edge of this kind of loose painting. It is super easy to add this splatter look. Just load your brush with color and then tap it gently onto your other hand (see image below). This will fling splatters of paint around the painting (and around your workspace, so be warned, this is messy!).

When you are happy with your watercolor art paintings, set them aside to dry.

Step Four – Remove Rubber Cement

Once your painting is completely dry (I mean completely dry! This is important to avoid smearing and smudging your work.), you are ready to remove the rubber cement. I found the best way to remove the rubber cement is with a clean, quality eraser. Just rub the eraser over the rubber cement and reveal your beautiful, finished design.

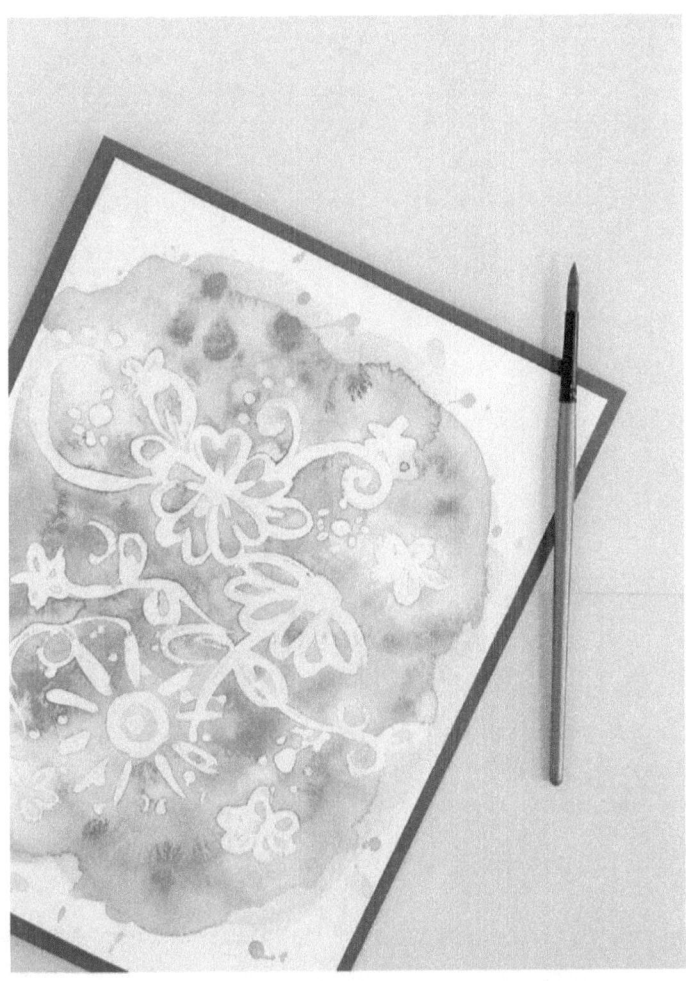

FORSYTHIAS

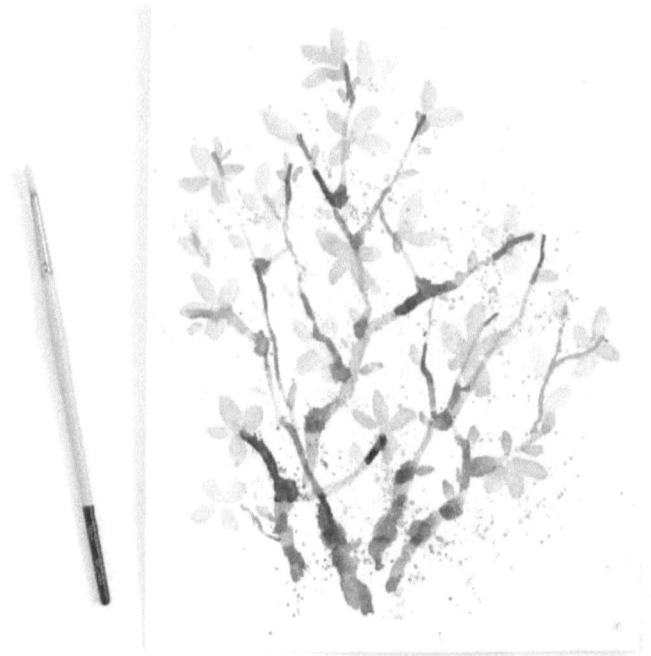

Materials and tools –

paper : Canson watercolor paper.

brushes: I like using brushes with a nice pointed tip for watercolors, they are great for washes, and for finer details

watercolor paint : you don't have to buy the most expensive kinds to start painting . There are many good watercolor sets for budding artists. A white plastic plate is also great for mixing colors

a dish to hold water for wetting and rinsing brushes

a straw! =)

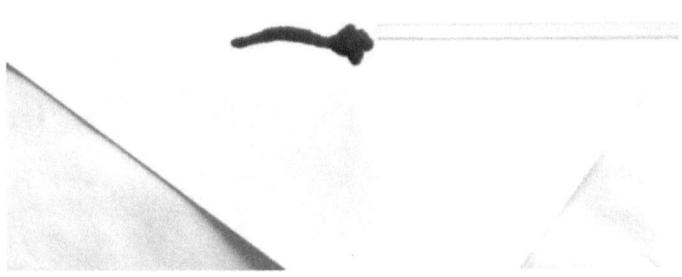

First, we are going to paint the branches.

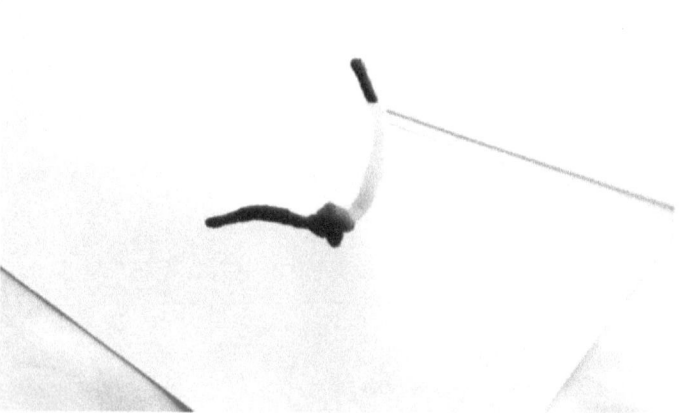

Start by making a puddle of deep brown color, then blow on the little puddle with a straw.

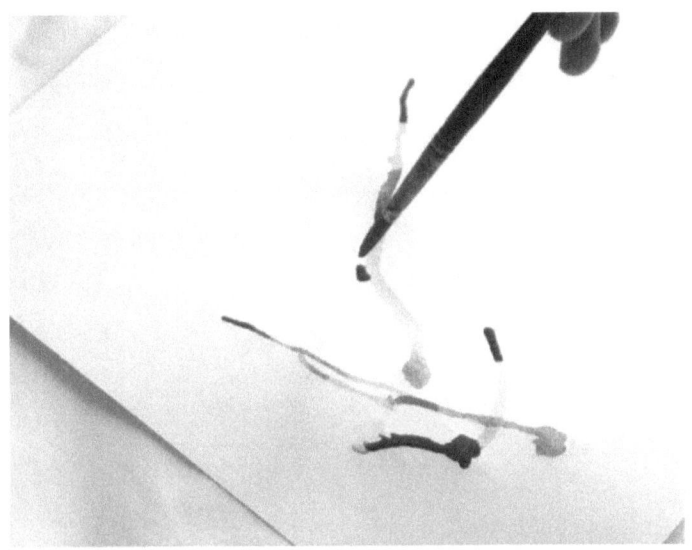

Repeat this process to create a few branches-

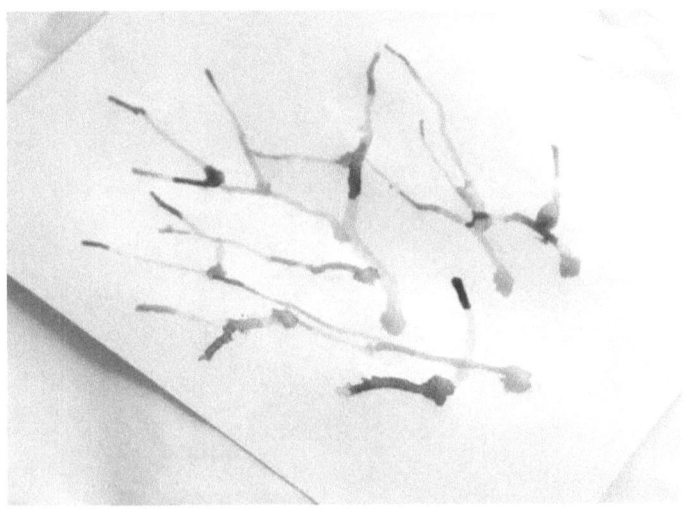

And more

Flower Painting With Watercolor

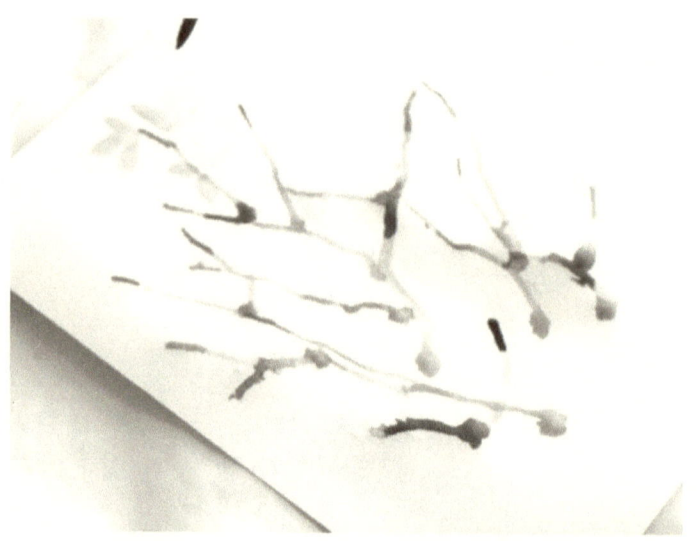

When all the branches are created, we can start painting the flowers and new leaves!

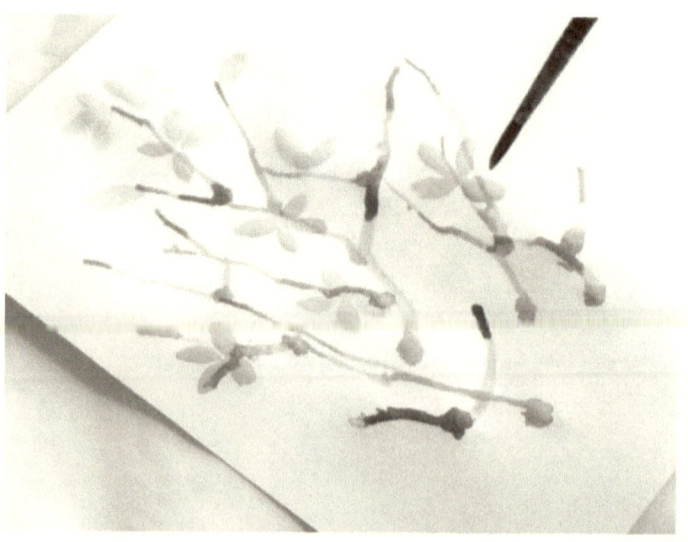

This is done with a brush.

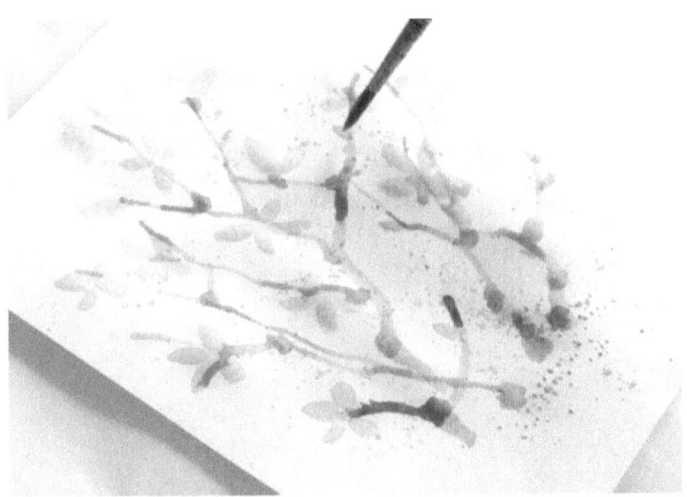

Forsythias have 4 petals, and the leaves are small, like all the new leaves of spring.

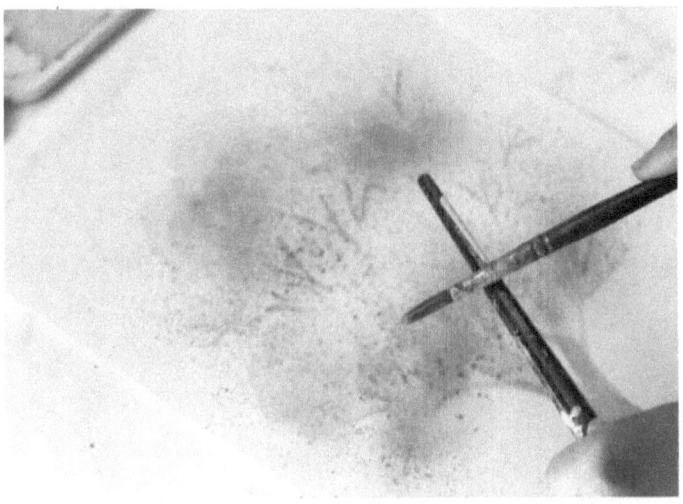

I also used the splatter paint method used in the watercolor fall tree painting!

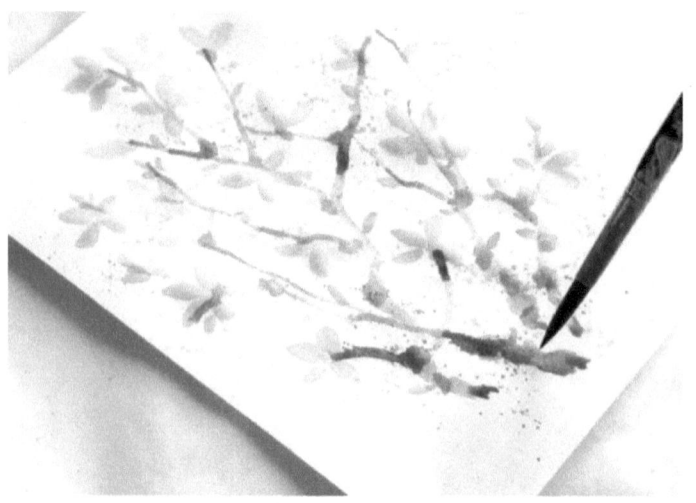

At the end, I added some deep brown color to base of the branches for more contrast.

Easy Watercolor Flowers

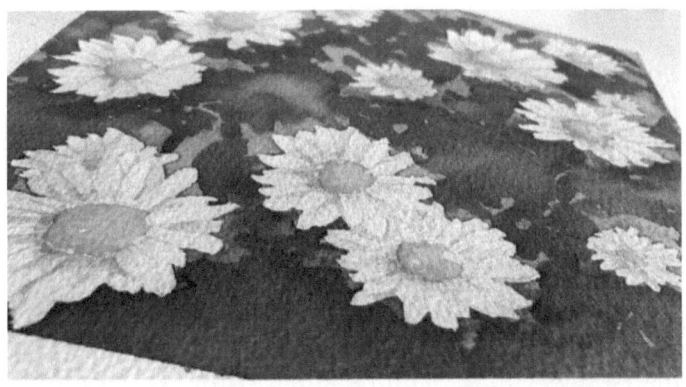

I'm going to explain in detail how to paint this flower composition, and I'll also teach you the vocabulary and techniques needed as we go along.

I've been painting with watercolor since I was a kid. But I'd by no means consider myself an expert. If I can do this, I feel confident you can do it too! And to help you along, you can download my template for sketching the exact same outline that I used for this project.

Becoming a better watercolor artist takes practice and patience. Above all I hope you enjoy the process of creating your own painting, and if you make a mistake, don't worry ! That's what learning is about. Just enjoy the process and next time you'll understand better what to do.

Watercolor flower techniques you will learn

This particular subject makes use of a number of techniques which you will use repeatedly when painting with watercolors. Learning the methods and the jargon whilst having fun doing some real painting is an excellent way to progress. So I'll do my best to explain the methods you're using so that you're painting and learning at the same time.

The techniques that you'll encounter during this still life project include reserving whites with masking fluid, wet on wet, glazing, and texture effects such as dry brushing, watersplatters and scumbling. We'll also go over some topics such as color harmony, composition, and values, which will contribute to your overall understanding.

About this flower painting

The subject is a cluster of bright white daisies on a background of green vegetation. I have tried to set up the composition of the painting so that the daisies are the focus of the painting whereas the background is designed to enhance them and make them stand out. This was achieved using contrasting values and distinctly different painting styles for the focal points and the background.

Let me try and explain...

Values or tone are an important part of any artwork. The term "value" simply refers to differences in tone ranging from dark to light. You can use values as a compositional tool when designing your artwork. Because your eye is naturally draw to the point of greatest contrast, you can create highlights and focal points by using highly contrasting tones next to each other.

This is why I chose to mask the flowers so that the white paper would remain untouched while painting a dark background. This method is known as "reserving the whites".

To further enhance the daisies as the focus of the painting I have painted them with hard edged detail (using glazing), whereas the background is painted in a loose abstract way. In a similar way to a photo which focuses on a subject while the background remains blurred and indistinct, this technique helps reinforce the subject.

The colors used for this painting use an analogous color design. Analogous colors are hues that are close to each other on the color wheel, (a color wheel is a very useful tool for designing color compositions and understanding watercolor mixing). In this case we have greens, yellows, and yellow-orange colors.

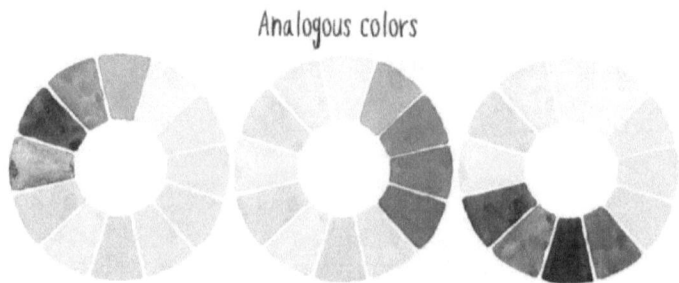

Analogous colors

Analogous colors like these produce a harmonious gradient of hues. They are often found in nature and are said to be perceived as calm and soothing.

The paint colors used for this project were as follows:
Phthalo blue (GS) + New gamboge. Together they mix a nice bright

sap green.

Phthalo blue (GS) + Raw Sienna. When mixed you get some nice dark greens.

Raw Sienna + Phthalo Green. Together these produce a medium leafy green.

New gamboge + Pyrrol Scarlet. This was used for the orange centers of the flowers.

Quinacridone Pink + Phthalo Green. Mixed together in a very diluted blend to produce a light grey color.

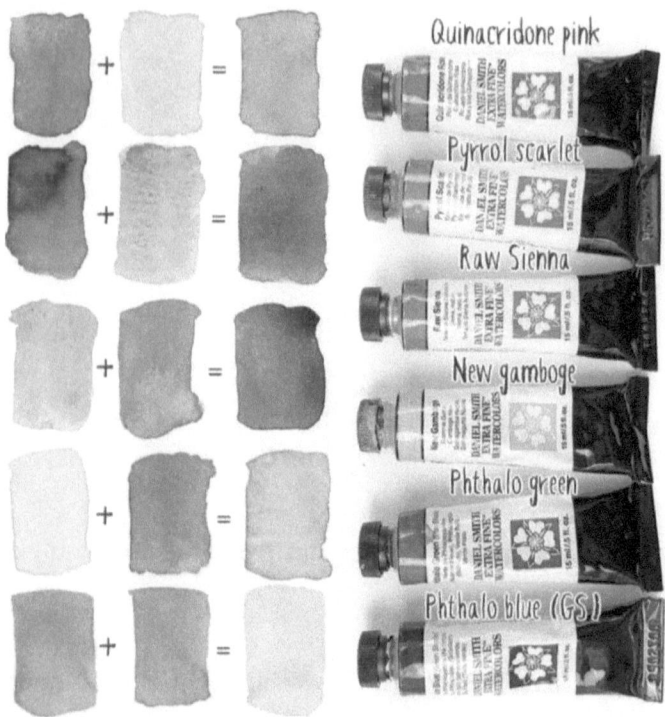

These six colors are enough. If you don't have exactly the same, try to use an equivalent. The most important thing is to keep the color temperature the same. For example Phthalo Blue (GS), Phthalo Green, and Quinacridone Pink are all cool colors. The others tend to be warm. If you're having trouble choosing which watercolor paints to use, feel free to take a look at my recommendations.

How to paint watercolor flowers step by step

Step 1 - Getting prepared

Begin by clearing a good amount of space on a flat surface near to some natural light if possible. I find that an uncluttered workspace makes the process so much easier. Do your painting at a time of day when you can be calm without interruptions. Switch off your phone and ignore the world for a while…

Here are my suggestions for the material you should use for this project:

Watercolor masking fluid.

You'll need this for masking the white flower petals during this project. This stuff is incredibly useful so if you don't have any I highly recommend it. It's not expensive and will be a good addition to your painting tools. Masking fluid (sometimes called frisket or even drawing gum) is basically liquid latex. Watercolor artists use this trick often because it makes painting background washes so much more simple. There are lots of different brands available. Winsor & Newton make a good product and Pebeo Drawing Gum is much appreciated by artists because it's colored to make application easier.

Find the right brushes.

Round brushes are all you will need for this painting. Ideally a medium and a small size. I used a round number 8 (silver black velvet) for most of the project and a smaller sable number 2 for the details. You'll also need a small brush for applying masking fluid, preferably something which you don't mind if it gets ruined !

Use the right paper.

Watercolor paper is a must for this project. You'll get the best results using 100% cotton paper, but use whatever you can afford, so long as the paper is quite heavy. The paper is going to get soaked when you paint with a wet on wet technique so you need something which can resist a large amount of wetness. I used 300 gsm / 140 lb Arches watercolor paper for this exercise.I would also recommend you use cold pressed paper. This has a slight texture and is probably the easiest watercolor paper for beginners. Rough papers can make smooth brush strokes more difficult, and smooth hot pressed paper is unforgiving because it tends to show up any flaws.

A board for attaching your paper.

You'll need a flat rigid board for fixing down the paper while painting. there are lots of alternatives you can try, such as marine grade ply board (resists warping well), hardboard, or gator board which is lighter. I also use a lightweight drawing board which I coated with marine varnish. Perspex sheets are also a good option which I'll discuss more below.

Two jars of water.

Mason jars a great for this, but be sure to have two jars. Like that you can use one for rinsing and another as your supply of clean water. It's good to get into the habit of using a clean water jar so that your watercolor paints don't get contaminated with other colors when mixing.

Step 2 - Transferring the drawing to watercolor paper

There are various ways to transfer a drawing to watercolor paper. You can use graphite transfer paper to trace an outline onto the paper surface. However, I find this leaves excess graphite of the surface and can get messy. Most of the time I just trace up against a window when the conditions are bright enough, or sometimes i use a light table. It was a dull day when i did this project so i used a light table for tracing.

I generally sketch my work on a separate sheet until I'm happy with the drawing, then I trace them onto watercolor paper using a HB pencil using thin pencil lines which won't show up after a few washes. Even if some of the pencil shows through I don't mind - it adds to the character of the artwork.

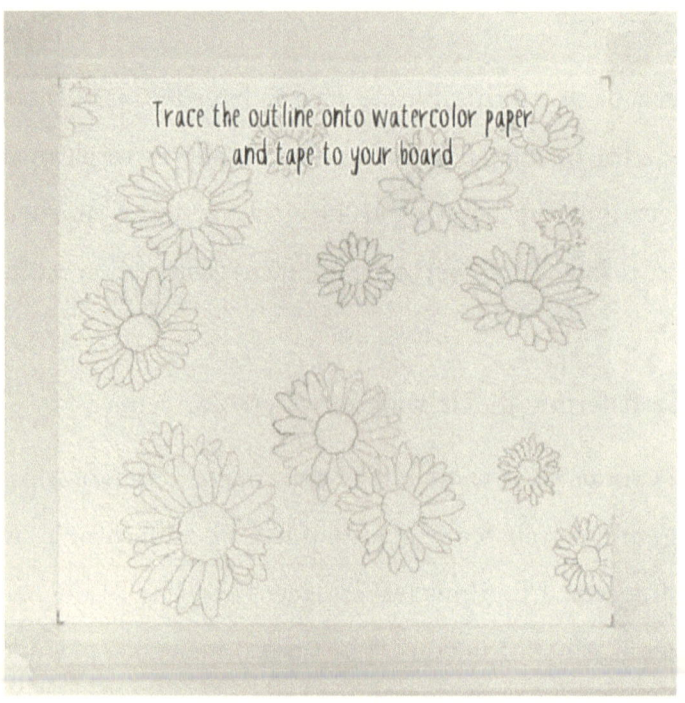

Step 3 - Fixing the paper to a flat board

In general this stage should be after the drawing transfer. For example, if you transfer using a light box, and if you're using a wooden board, then you can't tape down your paper until you've finished tracing. The problem with this method is that your paper will probably buckle because of the wet washes.

To overcome this, I suggest you use the heaviest grade of watercolor paper you can.

640 gsm / 300 lb is almost like card and you can still see through it with a lightbox. 300 gsm / 140 lb is a minimum weight. It may buckle slightly when painting, but it should straighten out a little when it dries.

Another alternative which I sometimes use when I have time to prepare is to use a sheet of clear perspex as my watercolor board. You should be able to find this in a good hardware store. It's rigid and transparent, so you can stretch your paper first, then do your drawing transfer second !

By the way I'm using low tack frog tape to secure my paper to the board - this stuff is great because it doesn't rip the paper when you remove it.

Step 4 - Cover the flower shapes with liquid masking fluid

Reserving whites is a necessity in watercolor painting because any highlights or white areas come from the white paper itself. You can preserve a white shape by painting around it, but when the shapes are complex, the easy option is to use masking fluid

There are various tools for applying the masking fluid, but for this project I used a synthetic brush which was specifically designed for masking (whatever you do don't use your good brushes for this). A small sized brush has the advantage of being accurate for painting small flower shapes.

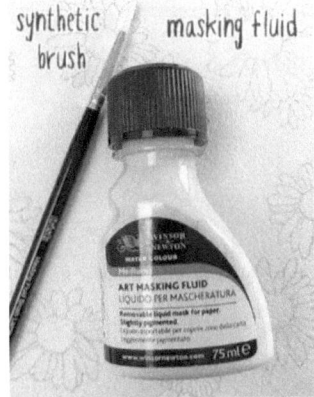
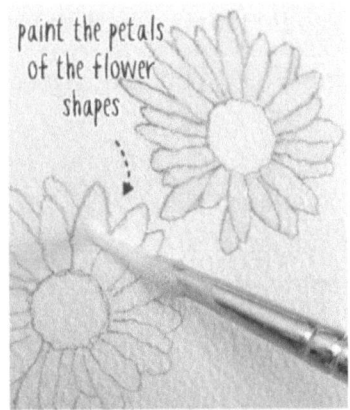
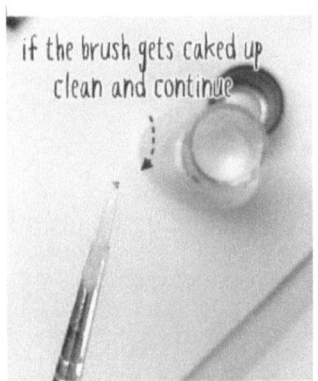
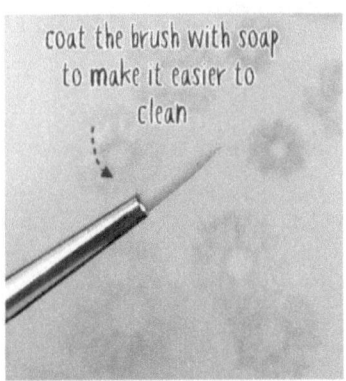

Mask all of your white petals but leave the yellow centers of the flowers so you can fill them in while the masking fluid is still on.

Leave the masking fluid to dry a few minutes before going on to the next stage.

Tips: You could try coating the tip of the brush with soap before using the masking fluid, This tends to make it easier to clean the brushes afterwards.

Also, when you do this phase of the project it's best to do the background painting immediately after the masking fluid is dry. If you leave the masking fluid on too long there's a small risk that it will stain the watercolor paper.

Step 5 - Paint a light toned wet on wet background

Wet on wet is a watercolor technique for producing beautiful blended colors. It literally means painting onto a wet surface.

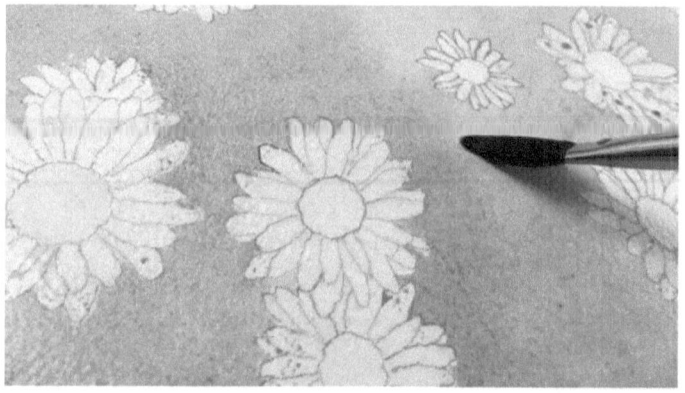

Keep in mind, this stage needs to be painted quickly before the paper surface has time to dry. It's a good idea to mix your colors first to save time. I used a light sap green and a darker leafy green.

Begin by dampening the whole of the background with clear water using a clean brush. Try to do this evenly without leaving puddles of water. Next, load your brush with some sap green and charge the wet paper with paint. You can paint unevenly so that you get patchy areas of lighter and darker tones. Try to make the bottom of the painting slightly darker by adding more pigment than the top.

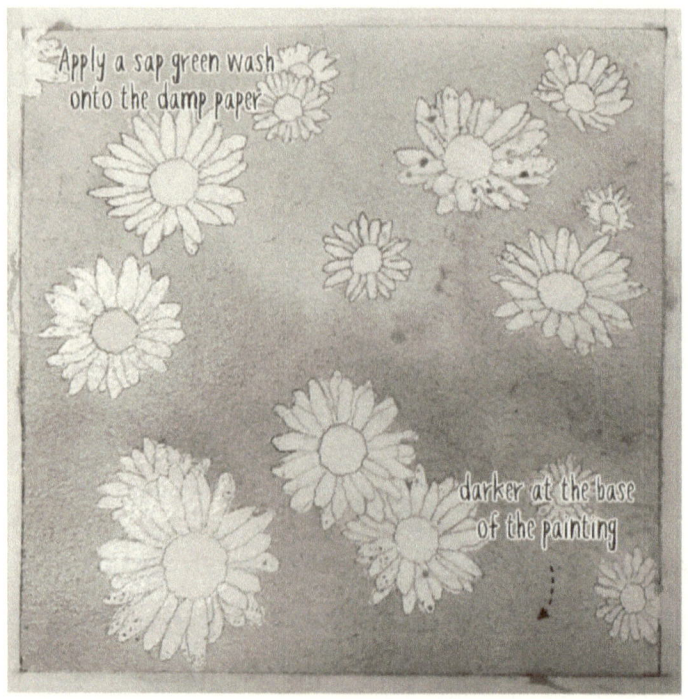

Now you can load your brush with darker paint and add some darker tones around the bottom edges of the flowers and the base of the painting.

Finally rinse your brush and load it with clear water. Flick the brush a couple of times over the painting so that drops of water fall into the wet wash creating splatters.

Splatters with clear water add texture to a wet wash, but the technique can also be used with a brush loaded with color.

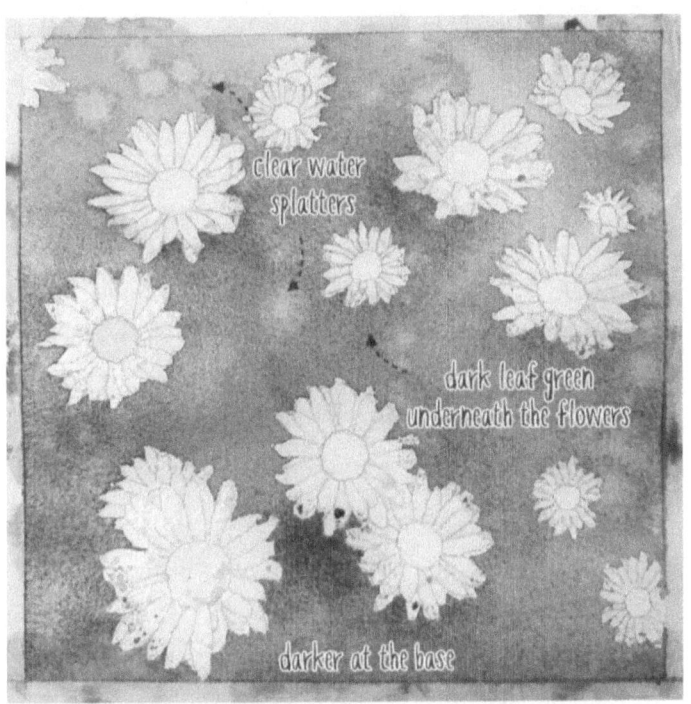

Step 6 - Paint the center of the flowers

Using a mix of pure New Gamboge, paint the yellow centers of the flowers, but don't fill them in completely. Leave some of the white paper untouched. I'm imagining the direction of the sunlight to come from above on the right hand side. With this in mind I tried to leave some white highlights in the yellow centers in the upper right hand spot.

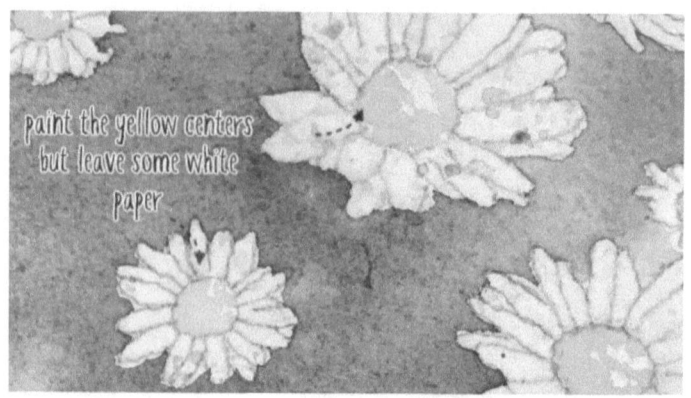

Step 7 - Add a dark toned wet on dry background

This is where you need a little patience. You need to let the wet background dry before moving on to the next stage.

Take a break, make yourself a coffee, and congratulate yourself on the progress so far!

When your painting is dry, mix a new dark green color. We're going to add another layer of paint to the background using a technique known as glazing. The term glazing means "layering" paint on top of an already dry wash. This is a wet on dry technique which means you must paint on a dry surface.

Laying down successive layers of paint increases the richness and deepens the tone of your watercolors.

The aim is to create a background which suggests leaves and vegetation without accurately painting any detail. Load your brush with dark green paint and brush around the flowers, being careful not to touch the yellow centers. Paint using random brush strokes in a haphazard way. This technique of painting is known as scumbling. It's a bit like scribbling with your brush.

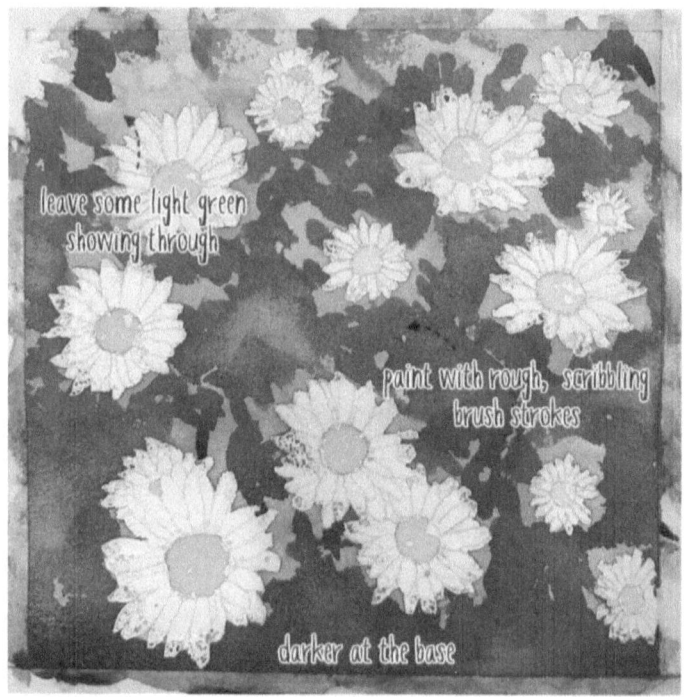

The idea is to leave some of the previous lighter background visible. Try to add more paint to the base of the painting and leave more of the light background visible at the top.

Tips: I have to admit I do sometimes cheat and use a hair dryer to help the paint dry quicker.

Step 8 - Remove the masking fluid

Leave the last wash to dry completely. You can now remove the masking fluid for the final part of the exercise.

I find the easiest way to do this is using a kneaded eraser (sometimes called a putty rubber). This is a pliable eraser that you can be shaped by hand for more precise erasing and has the advantage of not leaving any residue when erasing.

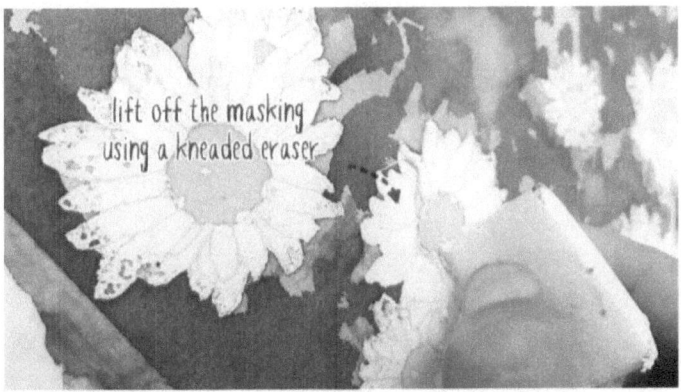

Use it in the same way as you would for removing pencil marks. It will help lift the dried masking off the paper to reveal crisp white flower petals underneath.

Step 9 - Add detail to the petals

Now you can add some details to the petals. Mix up a very light grey color (for example using Quinacridone rose and Phthalo green). Make sure your paint is very diluted and thin to get a light toned grey. If you're paint is too thick the effect will look exaggerated.

Paint the edges of the petals and add some shadow to some of the rear, overlapped petals to give a sense of depth. Use your pencil outline as a guide and paint these details wet on dry. You can use glazing to add additional layers of grey to reinforce shadows where you think they're needed. For example I put grey shadow on the left side of the yellow flower centers.

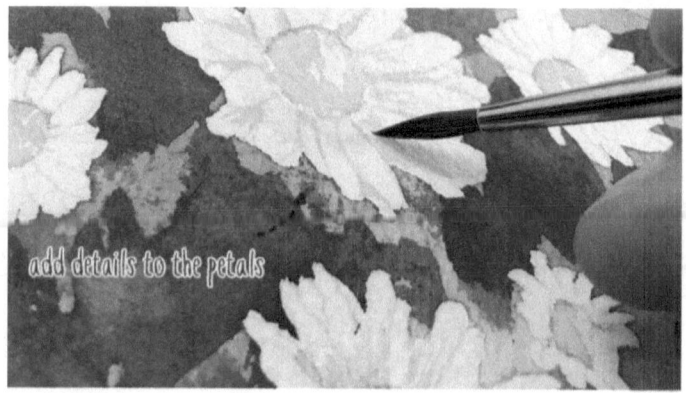

Step 10 - Complete the final details

Mix some orange paint to add shading to the yellow centers. Paint the edges of the flower centers on one side only to give a sense of three dimensional form.

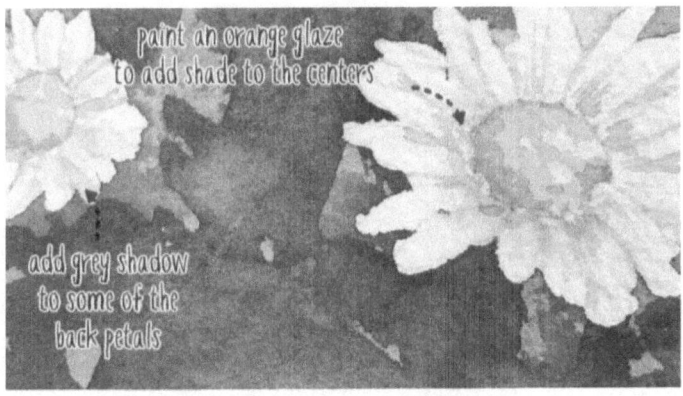

That's it ! Leave your painting to dry and then remove the paper from the board, being careful not to rip the paper surface. If you're using low tack masking tape you should be fine.

MAKE BUBBLE PAINT FLOWER HYDRANGEAS

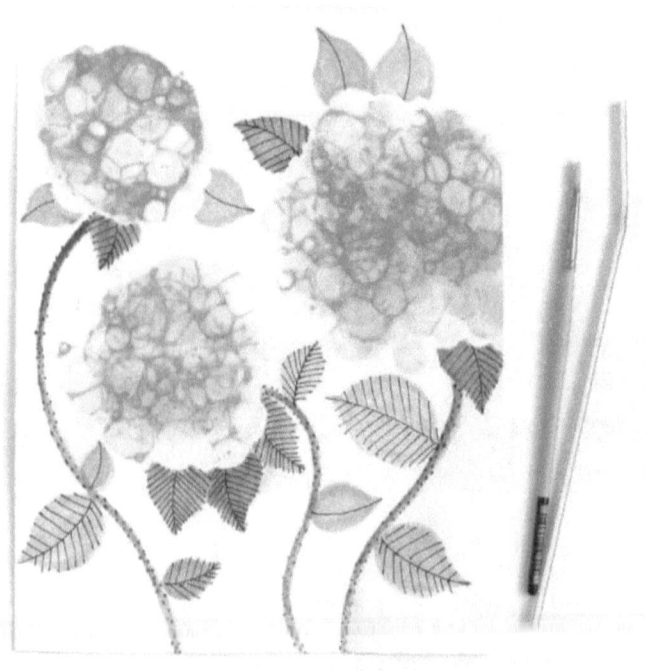

Materials:

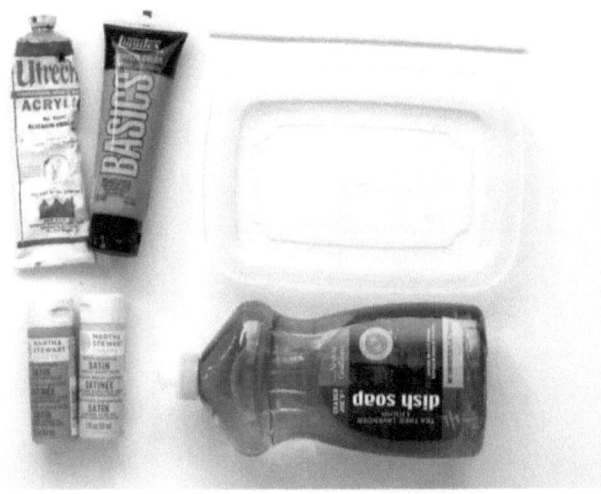

First, the bubble paint recipes- use paint and dish soap that are labeled Non Toxic !!

You can buy bubble paint, but it's very easy to make your own! I tested a few mixes, and the one I am really happy with is 1 part (by volume) acrylic paint, 1 part dish soap, and 2 parts water. Mix them up, that's it! (Some of the helpful resources are affiliate links.)

Find a dish to mix the paint. Mine are about 6"x9", and 2" deep.

I used this cardstock, which held up great! Now let the fun begin!

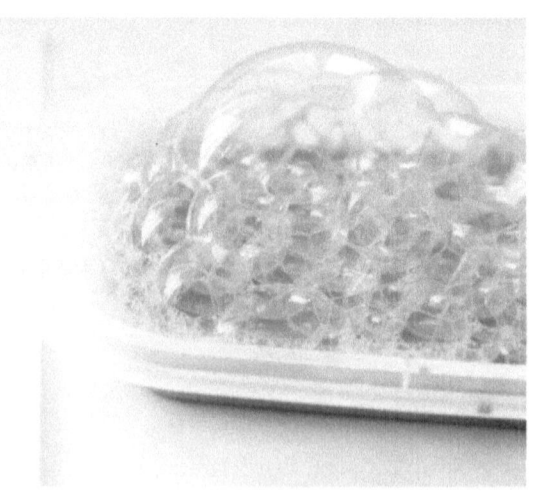

When you get a clump of fat bubbles (I don't need to explain how to do that right?) take a piece of paper and press it onto the bubbles. You can repeat a couple of times to get the desired shapes and colors!

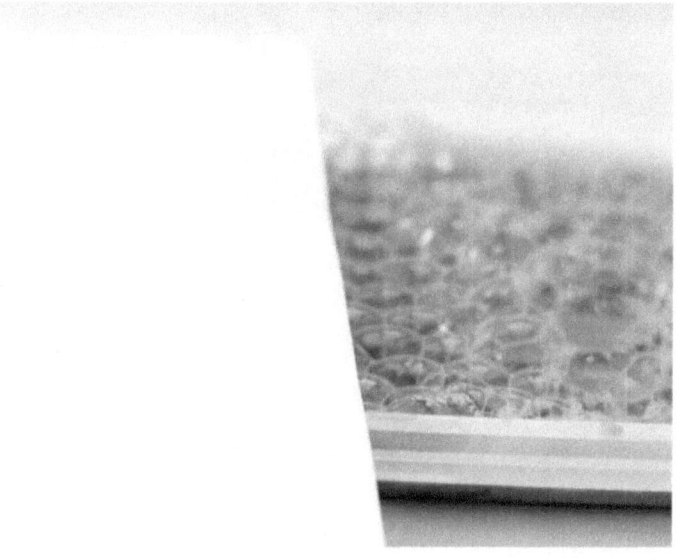

A shallow dish works well because the bubbles can come up easily, and when we press the paper onto the bubbles, the paper won't touch the rim of the dish and cause smudging.

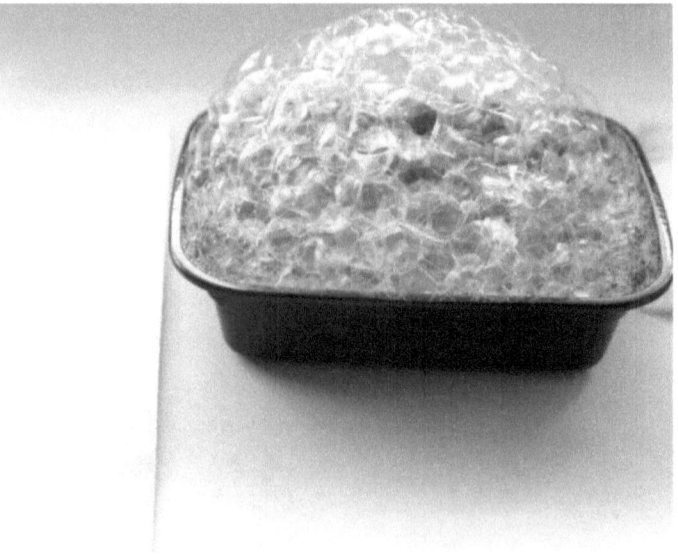

I used 2 colors here, one dish has rose pink, the other purple.

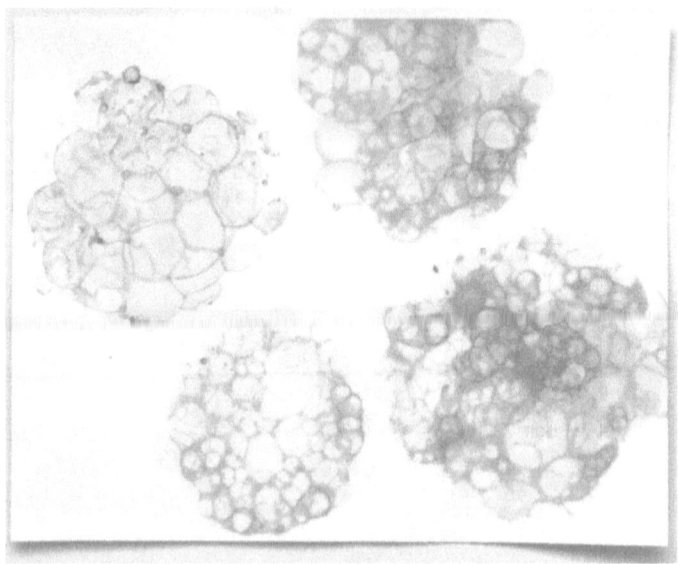

Now our Hydrangea flowers are starting to take shape!

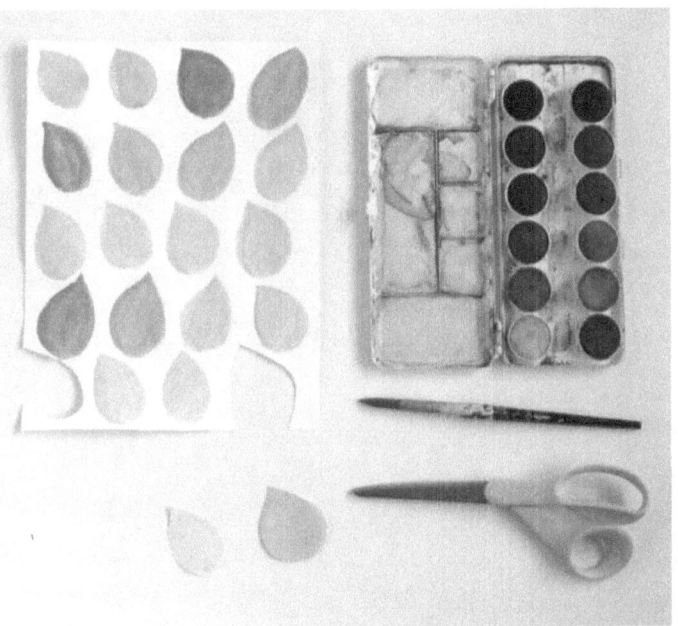

For one of the paintings, I painted some watercolor leaves in various shades of green, cut them out and glued them around the blossoms.

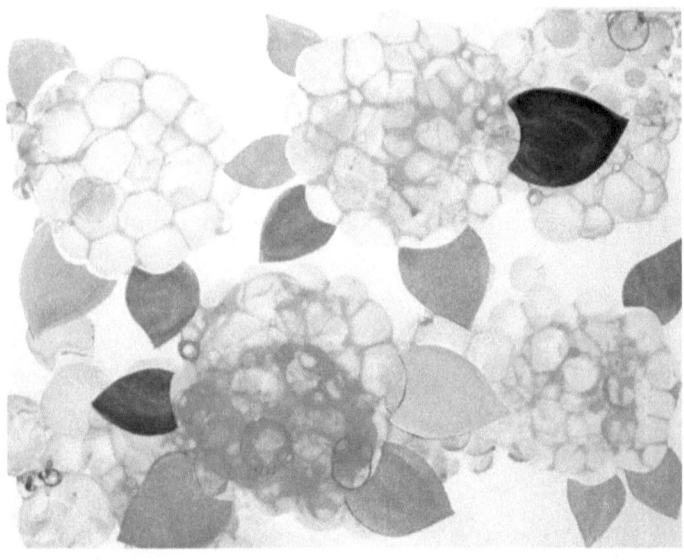

The other painting was completed by adding stems and painting a few leaves with water color.

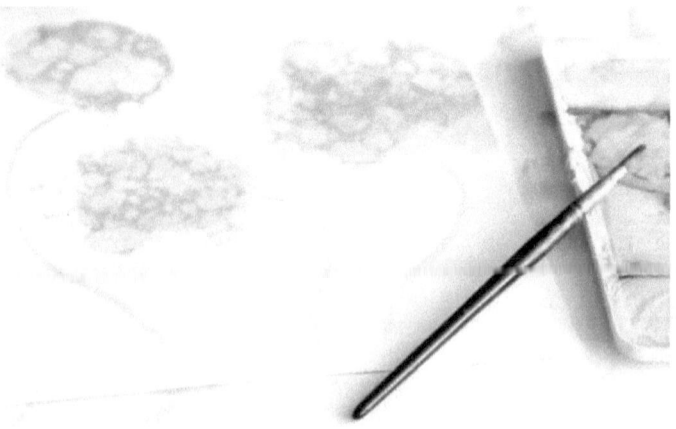

I like using brushes with a nice pointed tip for watercolors, they are great for washes, and for finer details.

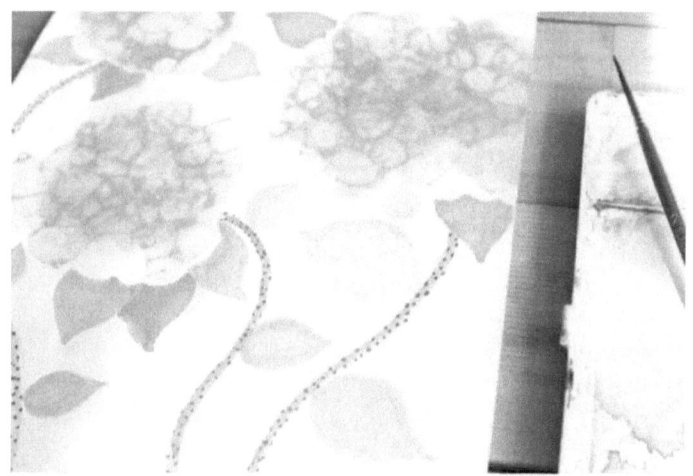

I felt the leaves need to pop a bit more, so I used a pen and added some rich details in both paintings, super easy though, just draw some lines!

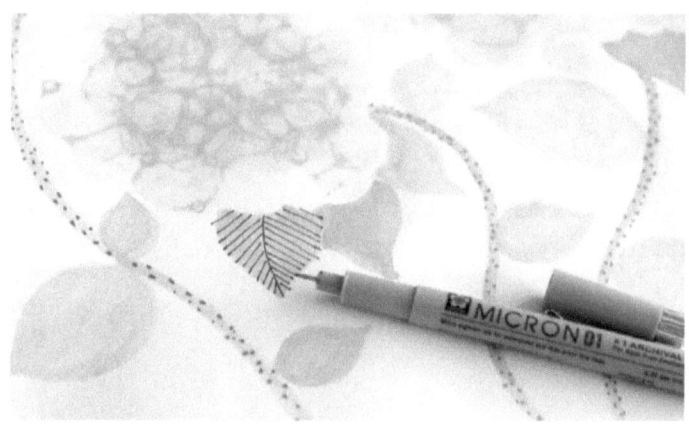

My favorite art pens! I used #01 here.

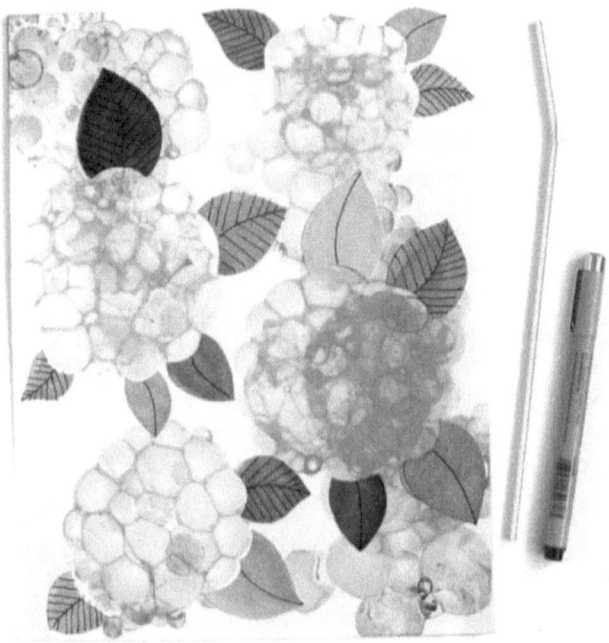

www.ingramcontent.com/pod-product-compliance
Lightning Source LLC
Chambersburg PA
CBHW030500220526
45464CB00006B/2591